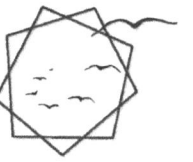

Poetry Collections by Stanley Paul Thompson

The Stork and Other Early Poems

Troth & Rapture: 400 Sonnets

Sonnets of Life Well Spent

The Stork

The Stork

AND OTHER EARLY POEMS

STANLEY PAUL THOMPSON

The Stork and Other Early Poems
Copyright ©2019 Stanley Paul Thompson

ISBN: 978-1-949652-03-1
Publisher: Mercury HeartLink
Printed in the United States of America

Rose photograph on back cover by the author; the Stork photograph by permission of Carroll Mae Springmeyer, her daughter Diane Pacolt and friend Janine Sahagian.

All rights reserved. This book, or sections of this book, may not be reproduced or transmitted in any form without permission from the author. Permission is granted to educators to create copies of individual poems for classroom or workshop assignments. with proper credits.

Contact Stanley Thompson at:
stan@shellmonster.com

Mercury HeartLink
www.heartlink.com

The Stork

Introduction   XVII

ONE

Tell my Heart	3
If You Need of Me I Will Come	4
You Left Confused	5
Did I Steal Away	6
How Love Is Won	7
Lost Memories	9
You Walked Into My Mind	11
Where Do Your Tears Go	13
Am I A Fool	14
Where Does Love Go	15
Green Parrot	16
Love (in Sandburg's style)	17
Tired of Love	18
Do They Even Suspect	19
Tonight I Shall	20
Aging Is Fun	21
Time Passed By So Fast	22
I'll Hold This a While	24
"I'll Hold This a While", Addendum	25
New Mexico Fall	27
My Persistent Cat	28
A Writing Fool	29

Saturdays	31
The Life I chose	32
The Mood is Right	34
I've Searched	36
Wonderings	37
A Truth Tonight	39
Sunrise Dew	40
My Poems	41
Sanctuary	42
I'm Not Sure That I Should Tell You	43
The Opalescence of Dawn	44
Floyd Pays a Visit	45

TWO

Growing Older	49
Mystery No. 1	50
In My Prime	51
A Shakespearean Proposal (in Modern English)	53
Fireflies in the Dark	54
A Romanticist at Heart	55
Never	56
If I Live to be a Hundred	57
The Ratcheting of Guns	59
You Are No More	60
The Lighthouse	61
Tonight the Quail Came Home	62
Home of Forgotten Dreams	64

Night Creatures	66
You Can Never	68
He Sang a Poignant Ballad	69
When We Will Meet Again	70
Don't Buy China Items	71
The Art of Feeding a Cat	72
A Lasting Poem	74
Angry Old Man	75
Happy Old Men	76
Cycle of Life	77
Feeling Safe	78
So Lonely Is Despair	79
Loss of Energy	80
A Word	81
A Word (translated)	82
How Does Love Die	83
Twixt Two Settings	84
I'm Having Fright	85
My Repose	86
Did it Rain Today	88
I Take So Much Joy	89
The Feeling Deeds	90
You Can't be Mean and Be A Poet	91
Frayed Cuffs	92

THREE

They Write to Cross Swords	97
The Fallow of My Life	98

Worth Some Exaggeration	99
The Inner Me	100
A World Below	101
It Came With the Rain and Wind Last Night	102
She Moves Oh So Slowly	103
The Pat, Pat, Pat	104
A Simple Poem	105
Go Rest, Congeal	106
Reaching a Turning	107
Free Falling	108
Rescue Me	109
A Bad Arrow I Aver	110
Knowing Your Cat	111
Why A Title	112
New Mexico Snows	113
The Stork	114
I Will Champion Loving	115
Explaining Death of Grandma to a Child	116
Patterns	117
Memories, the Opium of Old Men	119
Gooseberries	122
Random Thoughts	124
A Grandeur Christmas Gift	125
A Sinuosity	126
Dark Haunting Eyes	127
They Become the Salve	128
Poems From The Womb	129
Affaire d'amours	130
Something More Mellow	131

Something More Mellow	132
All Multiphasics	133
Slip Away or Ship Aweigh	135
Reflection Time	136
Ever More	137
Forsaken	138
At Dante's Tower	139
My Last Rose of Summer	140
Those Subtle Changes	141
Ink, Pen, and Paper	142
Day Dreaming	143
A Silly Rhyme	144
A Poet's Daydream	145
She Comes a Twittery Way	146
They Buried My Soul Yesterday	147
In God's Eye Equal	148
Lover's Kisses	149
Believe Thou Me, the Trinity	150
As if She'd Been Liable	151
You're a Crooner Mister T	152
I've Wrote in Poems	153
Five Senses	154
The Irish	155
ABOUT THE AUTHOR	159

Introduction

I will start at the beginning, chronologically placing my selected poems from mid-September, 2011 to the last day of December, 2011. Thus these poems will reflect my thoughts as I pass through the days of the Fall of 2011.

There are some gaps; I have not included poems about my late wife of 50 years, poems that engage conversations with Elf and references to Cats that haunt the book shelves of the Black Cat Book Store in Truth or Consequences, New Mexico.

I'm noticing that I'm putting more into my poems too. But I haven't gone to strict cadence as I do in November and December. I've decided to add some comments on selected poems to give you the reader some insight into my thoughts while writing these poems.

Lost Memories is the first of three poems where I discuss the loss of human physical attributes. This one is about memory. What got me started with this poem; more prose perhaps; was a picture of my father, Harold Stanley Underdahl Thompson when he was in high school in Faribault, Minnesota Many old photographs taken where names are all but forgotten. The other two poems are **Where Do Your Tears Go** and **Where Does Love Go**.

Love (in Sandburg's Style) is about Sandburg's break with the usual crowd of poets and started writing prose, not bothering with rhyme or meter in any exact manner. It is much easier writing poetry this way, at least for me and that maybe why so many modern day poets write in a similar fashion. I like this poem, especially the last stanza; "Your caress, light fingertips trace roadmaps to me". This poem could be about anyone.

Sunrise Dew is a cute poem. This is perhaps the first time I've mentioned Sprites. They become the rogues in my later poems. When I read the first line of stanza one I think of Josh Groban singing his song; "Bells of New York City". I don't think I had that CD when I wrote this poem. I find with this poem I am using phrases and words carefully.

The Opalescence of Dawn; I have to explain this title as I hadn't thought that it might be something different. In fact, I coined the word, made it up, poet's license, you name it. And I like it very much. It is not in any particular meter however. Ok, opalescence means (in my minds dictionary) multicolored, like Opals. So dawn, sometimes when atmospherics allow, glows in multicolor. You get the idea. As to the meaning of the poem, it shows my rethinking something's, more of coming to grips with reality.

Mystery No. 1; few have guessed the mystery answer so I'm loath to give it here. Perhaps readers will e-mail me with their guesses. **Never**; this was a new form for me. Rhyming the single word of each two line stanza. **Home of Forgotten Dreams**; Kind of a play on words. Katherine Jenkins, soprano in her album, *La Diva* sings a song titled House of No Regrets. I liked that name so this one may have come from subconscious. Not a farfetched idea of archiving stories of seniors.

You Can Never; this is not about me. I had written down the title and that night I wrote this poem. All of the things are true too. I like this poem. **The Art of Feeding a Cat**; and an art it surely is. **So Lonely is Despair**; well now...was I really trying to compose a love ballad? I can read more than one answer. Perhaps it is best said that this poem is for all despairing lovers. **How Does Love Die**; this could very well be about a long lost love, perhaps at college; I'm not sure. My gut feeling says that I was intrigued by the title floating around in my subconscious. **I Take So Much Joy**; another of my short poems about Twinkie. It also reminds me to savor her as she is 12 years plus. Of course, she may be thinking the very same about me.

The Fallow of My Life; someone mentioned to me about being or knowing or someone in the fallow of their life. I replied that I had written a poem with that word in the title. The term 'fallow' comes from the farm practice of not planting in acreage for a period of time. So to understand this poem I am assuming that I have not been doing much in my later life. That may be stretching it a bit. But then, what I write does not necessarily mean that is a fact; I again cite poetic license. **Free Falling**; more on separating. A good poem in structure and use of words. Why it is that angst produces so many good poems? **The Stork**; you have to see the picture (which is on the cover) to understand this poem. Perhaps one of the best of my poems as it mixes just enough of silliness and truth, was this done in the style of Lewis Carroll's Alice? I am a great fan of this man whose real name is Charles Lutwidge Dodgson. *Affaire d'amours*; written for a love that is far away. Don't make me say who I think it is; it's for any lover separated by unforeseen circumstances.

My Last Rose of Summer; It may have been the singing of Thomas Moore's words by any of a number of my singers, like Fleming, the Celtic Woman, etc. I took a picture of my yellow rose and I sent it to my friend in Southern Minnesota. She doesn't read her e-mails so it may take a while before I hear from her. The picture of the rose is on the back cover of my book. **A Poet's Daydream;** now a single word. This may just be the best poem I have written. I spent a lot of time thinking about each word. I told Twinkie that this one might just win me a prize. Wishful thinking perhaps.

She Comes a Twittery Way; Written about my only grandchild, Maiah. I hope she will remember Grandma Pat. This poem, a fanciful episode, is more about my feelings. The fuddy-duddy part maybe true. **As if She's Been Liable;** I started with the first line that I had written a week before. When I began I was thinking about a broken romance, but then at the end of the first stanza when it appeared to be a matter before a court I thought of the woman in Iran (who now from news accounts is to be hanged instead of stoned). Anyway, this is the poem that came out. I used the 'He's' in the last line as she would not have been brought up to think otherwise.

The Irish; the last line, 'Any rancor' was what I changed; 'British rancor' was my first choice, but then thought what do I know about the problems these two countries face. It still rings true as the Irish have always been battling someone over freedom.

The Stork

One

Tell my Heart

Tell my heart to stop racing
whenever I see her near me.
Tell my memory to cease erasing
these moments; just let them be

Tell my eyes to gaze fondly
at her when she steps away.
Tell my lips to graze lightly
when I hold her and don't sway

Tell my voice to whisper sweetly
so only she hears me.
Tell my arms to hold her tightly
so she doesn't flee

And all these things I command
myself to allow.
And all these things I demand
to respond and happen now

September 16, 2011

If You Need of Me I Will Come

If you need of me I will come.
If you need my voice I will hum.
If you need my poems I will send.
If you need my love I will mend.

If you want me to write I will pen.
If you want me to love I will; when
If you want me to return I will appear.
If you want me to go I will disappear.

If you tire of me I will be here.
If you dream of me I will be there.
If you ask of me I will provide.
If you demur of me I will abide.

If you need some time I will wait.
If you need an escort I will date.
If you need of money I will sum.
If you need of me I will come.

September 19, 2011

You Left Confused

You left confused, your mind was questioning.
I sensed it as you left, the parting was painful.
We embraced and hugged; I felt your trembling.
A short kiss, but a kiss is still a kiss; mindful.

I told you that I loved you now; at this time.
You thought I was remembering out of the past.
I said no, it was this time and on this dime.
I wanted it to be remembered and not to be cast.

How can I end this when it has no ending
Does not love transcend the distance between us
Does love not go on and on without bending
I only ask that you allow my whispers to hush.

You left confused, but it will sort out soon.
The longing in your heart is pain you can bear.
I too shall savor loves separation boon.
I will be your strength in sharing loves tear.

September 19, 2011

Did I Steal Away

Did I steal away from you
and my going home makes you blue
I never meant to hurt you too,
but my leaving has made it rue

I'll make it better if you let me
write of love and pen amorously
poems that settle your beatenly
heart, and lull you into nothinglessly

I can only pledge my fondest love
to be sent racing to you by a dove
or, by the South wind coming from above
of my longing; that you can be certain of

Did I steal away from you,
making me the culprit; not true.
I can sit here writing words anew,
notes that will thrill you, poems that do too

September 22, 2011

How Love Is Won

I watched a great movie; "The Terminal",
starring Hanks and Zeta-Jones; film 7 years old.
I must be on a roll or something subliminal
has made me purchase these films; bold.

It's another love story, but not with a girl.
The love of a father's dream is what drives
the hero to subject himself to no peril,
but the security of an airport when he arrives.

I teared up in one scene, it's easy to locate.
Hanks is a great actor, a proven one too.
I'm not sure what lesson there is; investigate.
But it is another one she would definitely woo.

I've learned a great deal about myself
watching these many movies; I can't choose them.
It probably is hit and miss, although my elf
which guides me produces no ill or mayhem.

I've learned the abracadabra of passion,
no secret chamber or doings with mirrors.
Love can be learned from forbearance, submission
and patience; but not with impetuosity; errors.

Can love be won only with calmness; no.
Love is often dynamic; liken a sudden blow
that rocks your foundation, your alter ego.
But sooner or later composure rules; you'll know.

So I persevere in my loving quest;
the one I've chosen; she will see my truth.
For when it is accepted; no doubts, all at rest.
Then, in everlasting embrace; the ovation; we doeth.

September 23, 2011

Lost Memories

So many faces I observed looking outward.
The world at their door steps, were they anticipating
what lay ahead, these pictures of students looking toward
the camera, wondering about future participation.

This started me thinking about their thoughts
which would instantly be kept in memory accumulations.
What happens to their memory, are they just jots
of information, snapshots recording sights and emotions

Memory has been the focus of scientific study for years
and if you search: "where does memory go after
death", you will see many hopes, many fears
that memory survives in Heaven or dies in ether.

But what if memory was saved and we
just do not have the software to open it.
Would that be like going back in time, gee
movies have made that idea a box office hit.

I looked again at the picture of my dad
standing with his football buddies so long ago.
No record exists of his thoughts then, was he sad
or mad or just happy to be with friends, so-so.

What an interesting thought is the idea
of floating memory logs waiting to be opened.
You could hear and maybe even see via
some yet to be discovered electronic gizmo; tokened.

There could be a charge too, enterprising business
that might even solve our fiscal problems.
But, I digress, just to hear Napoleon's address
to his troops at Waterloo would be exciting; sob-less.

But if I could open a memory then whamo
someone else could also and that could be bad.
Maybe a lock system with passwords; mumbo-jumbo,
but who would set them; this is becoming a mess dad.

All I wanted was to hear your voice again
to tell me you loved me, not asking too much.
When I flew my jet down Shumway at ten
did you notice I'd done a loop? Ouch!.

My wonderful theory on memory saved is wacko
I know, but if it could happen, wow!
It's probably best to forget it. You know,
leave if for a future poet to invent and bow

September 24, 2011

You Walked Into My Mind

You walked into my mind
when I wasn't looking.
How do I talk to you,
do I need a booking

You stole my beating heart,
was that even possible
Do I need it now for love,
or is that impossible?

You blinded me with pyrotechnics
so I only can see your face.
Even when I close my eyes
I see you; I cannot erase.

You deafened my hearing too;
did that block your voice
If I try real hard I might
hear your whispers, nice.

You left me in a dummy state,
I can't even tie my shoes.
I hope this is all reversible;
can you give me any clues

I suppose they'll take me away,
lock me up as helpless.
What a job you've done here,
leaving me so selfless.

Is this what true love does;
corrupts the very soul
Does it continue on and on
or do I have to pay a toll?

You walked into my mind;
all hell broke loose, ring-a-ding.
But even with these affects you gave
I wouldn't change one thing.

September 25, 2011

Where Do Your Tears Go

I've wondered, where do your tears go
Running down your cheeks, leaving lines
that I can see, no hiding them, no.
They sparkle in sunlight; are there other kinds

When they fall and strike the ground
does the Earth soak them up too
I guess I've never observed or been around
to see if they did in fact do.

Maybe there is a special flower
that blooms when tears fall near.
Where does it grow; it must be somewhere
nearby, you only cried last night dear.

Or, maybe you caught them up
in a hanky or soft tissue.
That you cried; I heard them erupt
and pour in torrents; I had hurt you.

I'd give all I have to bring them
back to you, to dry your cheeks.
Your tears, so special, that I'll pen
a poem like Lord Byron or maybe Keats.

September 25, 2011

Am I A Fool

Am I a fool; my talk is of an idiot.
That I can write in prose or poem so fine
does not change my awkwardness for naught.
I get tongue tied, pauses on the phone line.

I dream as I write lines of love, unrelenting,
of pictures so beautiful, my eyes in awe.
When I talk to you my thoughts, macaronically
confusing even to myself, leave me with ahs.

If I could only have cue cards, or
maybe a teleprompter, I'd speak finer.
As a last ditch effort I could memorize for
you whole sentences or heavens, a one liner.

All of these gimmicks are not for me.
I'd rather send notes and poems as your cupid.
I'll write more and speak less, you'll see,
so accept me as a fool, but not stupid.

September 25, 2011

Where Does Love Go

I asked my Elf, where does love go
once it has been used up, vanquished
Her answer, another question; you know
love is given, but can it be taken back, extinguished

I suppose so if one breaks an engagement
that would be equivalent to taking love back.
But I still need to know its movement;
does it rest with memory; piggy-back

The Elf said I was going down the wrong road,
that I had tried this with memory and tears.
My rejoinder was that no one had tackled the load,
the tough philosophy required for study, perhaps years.

So I began my study, it took months.
I reconnected the Elf, she had moved.
Speaking circumambrage, the Elf was no dunce,
but I might wow her with verbiage shoved.

I began; love lives and dies many times
over a relationship, that is a given, *a priori*.
When one dies the other remembers love, sublimes.
When the other dies, relatives remember, savvy

The pinch happens when there is no one
to remember, then love floats free and nests
with poets, like me, to renew so none
of the love is ever lost; in eternity rests.

September 26, 2011

Green Parrot

Green Parrot of Genus Pionis sitting on branch,
you are one of many species, many colorations.
Found in Central and South America, I bet you launch
at any sounds loud to your ears; detonations.

And you are eyeing me that I can see.
You're not quite sure if friend or foe are you
Should I let him in to join, to be
one in my nest, or should I fly away, boo hoo.

So take your time, you gorgeous Green Parrot,
look me over, investigate at will, I'll not mind.
Should you decide I'm a foe, I guess I could bear it
but I'd rather you let me pet you, perch near, be kind.

I once heard of a Parrot much like yourself,
she'd perch away, waiting for that perfect mate.
And, one came by one day while at the delf,
then flew away never to return, such is fate.

You'll sit and wait at the quarry's highest ledge
or fly to subtropical vines and trees with fruit
to eat, perhaps a banana or bright leafy veg
to keep you healthy and looking so cute.

I now sense your wavering mind mulling
me over and over; is he, is he not; repeating.
Don't be like the Parrot I once heard of, culling
away, alone; just grab me as the one you're seeking.

September 27, 2011

Love (in Sandburg's style)

When I speak of love
am I remembering you.
Have you so denuded me
I can only speak that way?

When I think of love
my mind is stuck
on the search word: you.
I can't remember others.

When I write of love
my pen marches alone.
No direction can I impart
to change the address.

When I act in love
I feel only you.
Your caress, light fingertips
trace roadmaps to me.

September 27, 2011

Tired of Love

Am I tired of love
When heartbreaks I'm flinging.
When amorous bells I'm ringing.
And with me so much singing.

Is love tired of me
When love darts go missing.
When strange cats go hissing.
And when maidens stop kissing.

Is love all it meant to be
When I'm happy wantonly.
When distance shortens instantly.
And when you're with me constantly.

September 28, 2011

Do They Even Suspect

Do they even suspect
me of wanting love,
love that does not
appear, can't be seen

They pass by me in pickups
silently thinking
perhaps country music is played,
but do they suspect

When I work at the food shelf
hungry looks greet me.
They're not interested
in what I'm thinking.

So what is it they don't suspect
Am I weary, do I cry
at home, is there a death
that lingers on and on?

I shall pass my day
doing mundane things
but in my heart I know
it's your love, unseen.

September 28. 2011

Tonight I Shall

Tonight I shall sing praises to you.
Rich, deep baritone melodies they'll be.
My voice will carry swiftly in the sky of blue,
then to fall gently, ever so softly to thee.

Tonight I shall pray fervently, that God,
will protect you, will keep you safe, this I plead.
May God's angels watch over you, never to nod,
never to waiver, never to shirk their duty creed.

Tonight I shall write poetry so loving
that you may swoon, may feel light headed.
Poems deep in meaning, with words hovering,
then descending like Fall leaves to you, deeded.

Tonight I shall dream that I'm with you,
that we are walking hand-in-hand, happy
that the day is warming, that birds flew
above us, that our pathway is cool and vapory.

Tonight I shall carefully write you notes,
pages and pages, that thrill you, that make
you laugh, that tell of my sincere love; quotes
too if I like them, some to rock, but never quake.

Tonight I shall ask you to love me,
to be your favorite, your prince, forever.
And in return I will pledge, no, guarantee,
that I will be with you, to leave you never.

September 29, 2011

Aging Is Fun

Everyone eventually ages overtime.
A paunch here, a slouch there, everywhere
both sexes gain wrinkles, ain't it a crime.
And then there's the lack of attractiveness; be fair.

I've noticed too that one might even cheat
and with a surgeon's hand, camouflage aging.
But in the end, even that fails, just meet
Dorian Gray and you'll know the sin of waging.

What is aging anyhow; besides the wrinkling?
It is a pleasant experience in most cases,
car loads of memories filled with crinkling
Christmas presents, kids growing up, smiling faces.

I wouldn't trade my age for anything more.
I've gained so much, met adversity, dove in
and survived, became enhanced, didn't bore.
So join me in the fun, you'll be glad, we both win.

September 30, 2011

Time Passed By So Fast

Tonight on the phone, you wondered about your life,
how time has passed by so fast, it didn't last.
I too have the same thoughts; our lives are rife
with pleasant surprises, some disappointments, all happen fast.

But how wonderful to have those memories remain
inside of you, to be able to recall them when needed.
Our lives are filled with many facts, opinions, and the main
gift is our ability to give sage advice to others when heeded.

I'm sure a minute seventy years ago is still today
the same minute (the Earth spins constant) and so
something else is happening, maybe anticipation of day
to day events appears quicker, so time is shortened, no

Can you remember how you waited and
waited to become sixteen, it seemed to take
forever I recall, and then there was a wedding band,
children born (forever at age 2), waiting for a cake to bake.

Perception is a strange bug-a-boo, we think life
passes quickly because we have experienced so much.
Writing this poem (maybe 30 minutes) maybe iffy,
but it seemed to me to be shorter, a time touch.

I live for anticipation of events, but when they're
completed they're memories and my search I renew.
An instant in our life maybe a kiss, but bare
of never again, you can look forward to kiss number two.

Your ideas and thoughts appeal to me always.
I feed off of them, they provide inspiration too.
Please, never hold back any thoughts, however sideways
they may seem to you, I relish them, take cue.

September 30, 2011

I'll Hold This a While

Am I to wake up one morning and think
why oh why I didn't pursue her, ask her
to be mine for as long as we shall live, to drink
from the same table, to live together, to be near

I know my Elf; she would say: "give it
a longer time, make sure you're not acting
out a whim, a ricochet from grief", and yet
I ask why wait, why continue with soul wracking.

Should she opt out, or ask for more time,
I could accept, for at least then I tried.
The words: "what could have been", I opine
will be my epitaph should I never had pried.

But I haven't asked her to marry me.
She may have thought it was best, but no!
I simply thought it on the record, sort of a key
to where I stand, what I might pledge as so.

Don't make me spell it all out Elf,
I know your ways, you'll think it is too
complicated, and why not just leave yourself
some wiggle room, you know she already loves you.

In any case, Elf continued, let it at least rest
for a few more weeks; you're not going anywhere.
I find her logic irrefutable, but still the least
I do the lonelier I become, do I swear.

October 2, 2011

"I'll Hold This a While", Addendum

"Well, I told you so, you did not
listen to me." Said my Elf in a
slightly sarcastic elfin voice. "It took a knock
on your head to get some sense," she remarked; aye.

"You didn't consider her side at all,
just jumped in, not testing the water
to see hidden rocks," she said standing tall.
Don't badger me Elf; I'm still thinking about her.

So I jumped the gun, well lots of people
do that and it doesn't hurt them fatally.
Look, I didn't give her the ring and steeple
thing, I was just supposing anyway, to tally.

Elf replied tersely, "So now what are your
so called grand plans? You obviously have not
thought this through and you better not bore
me or her with drivel, platitudes, or some rot.

That's enough! I don't want to hear anymore
about it, just let me think for a while.
I acknowledge and understand the core
reasons behind her call last night, it wasn't guile.

Even though I didn't understand the Trust
I got the message, loud and clear, that marriage was taboo.
Such arrogance would I impart should I bust
in demanding she forgo promised income, that I will not do.

Do I recant all previous poetic appeals; no!
They were given and written from my heart to her.
But from this moment forth I will regain, I'll go
the way explained before; remaining her lover.

So Elf, not much has changed you see.
Marriage or some other attachment we will dismiss,
for love does not require lock and key.
I'll go and she will come, both on whims and bliss.

October 4, 2011

New Mexico Fall

I can think of many things joyous
this wonderful time in New Mexico fall.
My friends in church choir are not coyish,
they sing with exuberance, hymns on call.

And then there is the community chorus
with singers of all faiths that appears
each week for practice, or more, as
Pastor Joe requires; our concert nears.

Lovely weather too, the days are warm
but not hot, that's for summer fare.
Evenings cool down; don't let me alarm
you though as freezing days are rare.

The hummers have left for tropical sun,
and soon the winter birds arrive to eat.
Pine Siskins and Goldfinch keep me on the run
filling Niger seed feeders full, it's my treat.

Yes, this is truly a joyous time.
With so much to do I'm never blue.
So if you want to share in this clime,
give me a ring and I'll show you too.

October 6, 2011

My Persistent Cat

Twinkie comes in, her determination, wow.
She is loudly meowing (more a squawk),
which is to tell me; "I need food now, pow!"
I stare her back, reply, look at the clock.

Twinkie can tell the time, that I know.
She also knows sunlight and darkness.
Both signify times for feeding her now.
And, if I don't comply she simply makes a mess.

So when she just came in minutes ago,
I said; look at the clock, you can tell time.
It isn't five yet, go read the comic strip Pogo.
She turns to leave, her look rivals a mime.

What I need to do is install some sound,
maybe a bell or buzzer that will trigger
a response in her left lobe; your meal is found,
you can now silently eat and get bigger.

But I already know she understands,
she does it to spite me, my persistent cat,
hoping I'll drop everything, yielding to her demands.
She's worse than a w..., no I won't say that!

October 7, 2011

A Writing Fool

I'm a writing fool I guess.
Penning poems; I'm lucky; God bless.
When the mood strikes me I can write
three, maybe even more into the night.

Love poems I really work at,
for some I'll even tip my hat.
Of course you need someone dear,
someone you love or have loved here.

Animal poems I really enjoy
especially Twinkie, my cat; I toy
with her, blaming everything on her,
but then she hops to my bed, gives a purr.

There are novelty poems that relate,
you know, the kind that asseverate,
acquaint, annunciate, articulate,
disclose, divulge, enunciate and narrate.

For instance I might write of singing,
the church choir comes to mind; ringing
bells along with our melodious voices
we raise the spiritual mind; *Deo gratias*.

Then there are the wild things like snakes;
you write on snakes, why for heaven's sakes?
Floyd was a pet Rattlesnake we knew;
of course different ones over the years grew.

Music I listen to give me inspiration,
many poems allude to this stimulation.
I think the soothing music keeps webs
from forming in my mind; isolating fibs.

But love poems, oh how I can sigh
remembering events and moments passed by.
My skin prickles, I feel quite high
when I pen to you, my love, and why.

October 7, 2011

Saturdays

Saturdays has ended, has it for you too?
I thought about you, driving around
looking at the Fall display,
catching Maple leaves falling,
the air crisp; white mist from the breath you blew.

Did you think of me, wishing I was there?
I pictured me driving, seemingly disinterested,
but secretly watching you,
caught up in all the splendor
of golds, reds, oranges and browns in the air.

But Sunday is coming; I feel the punch
taking me away from my day dreams,
bringing me back,
getting my groove in tune
with choir, church and the ladies lunch.

Maybe someday I won't spend Saturdays alone,
that activities with you will fill
my waking hours
with fun and jocularity
as we romp and stomp through life as one.

October 8, 2011

The Life I chose

You probably know what it's like,
sitting at home waiting for those
scheduled tasks; breakfast, exercise bike
ride, feed cat, etc. It's the life I chose.

Doing these same items everyday somehow
makes living easier, more uniform too.
I can add chores, but don't screw up the show
or I become lost and start remembering you.

Where this is going is any ones wild assed guess.
I suppose there is an end game; I've penned
some poems on what I would accept, less
of course those that you want to end.

The problem with me is there is too much time,
and yet, there isn't much time; an anomaly.
I said I could do this; love by poetic rhyme,
but I may just run out of stanzas; I'm melancholy.

I suppose we could just be good friends,
but would I still send you many paged notes
and poems about love, our sharing, our mends
I guess I could to this but where's the votes

Maybe I will chalk it up; forget this poem.
I might be in this mood because of music,
the movie watched, Twinkie's yowling, my home
which needs fixing, a lousy salad dinner, that I'm sick.

Naturally it isn't any of these; it's my mind
working in a different direction than my heart.
Your position is gnawing away as I find
more ammunition, more reasoning to keep us apart.

I won't send this poem, it wouldn't do.
I'll keep it and some day critics will
use it to portray their grand thesis of you
and of me, but they'll find it only a bitter pill.

October 15, 2011

The Mood is Right

It's a grand night for writing poems.
I guess I could have said; "singing", but
that line has been used before; comes
from Rogers and Hammerstein's "State Fair" hit.

Back to my first line, tonight I may just
write four or five poems; the mood is right.
That ability (ask Elf) comes in spurts best
used quickly err it fades quietly into the night.

So tonight is "Choose Your Poem" show,
kinda like "There's curtain 1, 2, and 3".
I'm not saying I'm a TV game host now;
no siree, but it's more like "Please Call Me"

You want a poem about our country
OK, it might take too many stanzas to
write of all the ills, the miss-steps contrary
to good sense that I would offer to you.

Next caller; "How about a poem on sports"
Too much money for both owners and players
will ruin professional sports; why it purports
to be the common man's game is beyond sayers.

I'll take one more; "Write a love poem please."
Easy as 1, 2, and 3 that I'll be in love with thee,
that we will sail forever in our dreams, at ease
but not asleep for you will have time to kiss me.

This was an easy poem to write to night.
I could have gone on and on, but times a limit
and folks want to get tickets to "The Price is Right",
but first a commercial, it only takes a minute.

October 15, 2011

I've Searched

I've searched for items you put away
and I can't seem to find what I'm looking for.
Not that our home is so large, but pray
you might have found a secret passage door.

Where could you have put the king bed comforter?
Size alone would make me believe it's secreted
in a chest or a plastic storage container,
unless...you gave it away to Good Will where it's needed.

I had some 8x10 glossy photos of opera singers.
Did you toss them or are they buried in picture
albums and they just slipped through my fingers?
An old girl friend photo; you probably ditched her.

Missing are twenty or more music CD plastic boxes.
I've found many and Barb just stumbled on six more.
They must be in your studio hiding like foxes
chased by English huntsmen; or destroyed by war.

There must be other items that I'll look for too.
It's frustrating for me to spend so much time
searching for items, items you may have threw
away when you said you were clearing mine.

October 16, 2011

Wonderings

I sometimes wonder if I've played the fool.
That is, have I been lacking in judgment?
Looking in my mirror I might say I'm cool,
but if viewed objectively, I'd say I was obsolescent.

Perhaps you are correct in stating my perception
is based on an adolescent encounter of lust,
which may or may not have been the apperception
I had of undying love; wanting you I must.

So in my recent wonderings I'm portraying a Vetter
taking an unbiased view of my looking back.
It is also indisputable that I thought better
of you as years passed, but circumstances I lack.

But now that has changed for me as it did you.
I'm forgetting years gone by, concentrating on now.
And a fool I'm not, for wanting of love isn't taboo.
And love at any age is still permitted anyhow.

To calm my persistent fears of playing the fool
I must not dwell on the past for it lacks
substance, it is an illusion I envisioned, a stool
with uneven legs that vacillates my facts.

These are important moments for us both,
and I'm probably of the more titubant association,
but I can offer you more; I'm not loath
to new experiences, to new ventures, to new explorations.

Where do these poems lead me now?
Rereading them I see I've addressed our fears
of false love, of hasty promises, of my vow.
I'm still your partner, your lover for many years.

October 16, 2011

A Truth Tonight

Whisper me a truth tonight,
for I'm doubting everything you write.
And should you not whisper what's right,
then I implore you to go and not fight.

You said you loved me, sincerely,
and I believed you most dearly.
But now what you've done, I see clearly
that your promises given were surly.

Don't tell me I have misunderstood
you writings too; they weren't all that good.
And please don't whisper, it's the mood
I'm in, that it will pass too; that's rude.

And when you hold me ever so tight
I am hoping and praying that my plight
is not for naught, for you do love me, right?
So please whisper me a truth tonight.

October 18, 2011

Sunrise Dew

There is a south wind blowing tonight
bringing my love thoughts to you.
So open your windows to catch them bright,
err they are caught and swallowed by sunrise dew

For at sunrise when the morning dew is formed
all the uncaught thoughts are harvested by fairies
to be read for chantage that can be wormed
out of these thoughts for purposes most eerie

That you will catch my thoughts for you,
I have little doubt; you'll rob these pesky
sprites of their booty; they'll be vengeful too.
Perhaps next time I'll send them FedEx; less risky

 October 19, 2011

My Poems

Have you noticed that my poems
have changed in intensity; to deepen?
I don't want to signal that danger looms,
nothing of that sort; just a change, *tout de même*

I tend to spend more time in writing.
These 'great thought' poems; more drafting.
It could be that the messages are more biting.
Then again, I might only be carefully crafting

Perhaps we shouldn't overplay their meaning;
it could be that I only stress themes more.
You know I have Elf; she can be demeaning.
And then there's my soul; to anyone else a bore

Intensity thickens as the plot boils; trite.
Yes I know, but an element of truth in there.
In love poems, being rhapsodic isn't always right.
That the tenor or meaning often softens loves fare

I will continue to pen my poems à la carte.
Some will be fanciful and cute, while others
will explore loves greater or lesser part.
In all cases though, they're my poems, not mothers

October 20, 2011

Sanctuary

Every time my eyes glance at your picture
a rope tightens around my heart, dear.
I've held so much back that one day a rupture
will flood my soul with memories of despair.

I feel I'm coping, yet so abstruse it all seems.
Do others see this hidden camouflage in me
Are they talking behind my back; or are dreams
scripting my thoughts and saying what ought to be

Does all this silent lamentation come from being lonely
Is a chemical in my brain aiding my grief;
but in that case a medication to calm might only
further hide these dispirited thoughts with no relief.

But maybe all of this is normal; to be expected.
For I do have many days when melancholia is absent,
and my volunteer activities that I have elected,
do offer sanctuary; making these thoughts distant.

October 21, 2011

I'm Not Sure That I Should Tell You

I'm not sure that I should tell you
that every waking moment
I think of you is torment
when I believe love so meant
should erase all fears, yet be true.

I'm not sure that I should tell you
of my persistent longing
for us in pair belonging
to make this trip journeying
together, sailing out of view.

I'm not sure that I should tell you
that our time spent together
not trying to forget her
but loving always forever
is my pledge which you already knew.

I'm not sure that I should tell you
of winter's gift of snowfall
for snowmen, start with a ball
and Christmas stories recalled
but in truth, I'll give you these too.

October 24, 2011

The Opalescence of Dawn

I composed today a love poem
from my steadfast heart, err I fawn.
I assembled it as my thoughts roam
hither and yon seeking the opalescence of dawn.

For the brilliance of our days beginning
is but a beacon guiding me in thought.
All the celestial energy I am absorbing,
building my arsenal of poems wrought.

If God were my cupid I'd surely win
the affection from you in heavenly ways.
But God is not my cupid, never has been
and never will be all through my days.

For our love, as we view it, is earthly fare,
born in lust it mellows soon at dusk.
An instrument for possession, but beware
that love harnessed will soon use it's tusk.

So I composed with love today most kindly,
never intending to champion the match.
Our love now, no longer of lust, but fondly
I've approached you, awakening, hoping to catch.

And now with dawn's brilliance, I have energy,
I feel ever so confident, much more at ease.
To be finally united in thoughts, our synergy
blossoms, our love voids filled, never to cease.

October 24, 2011

Floyd Pays a Visit

This afternoon, following usual rest,
I opened the screen door on back porch.
There are two steps to deck and I'm just
about to step down when I spied Floyd; ouch!

Floyd was lying stretched out, not moving.
When he saw me he continued to crawl away.
There was a fisherman's glass ball he passed roving;
there he curled up, rattle saying, beware my way.

Barb was out in the guest or blue room.
She calls it that because the walls are painted blue.
Makes sense; few guests I have needing bedroom.
Barb was resting, but getting up; I said, Floyd's about too.

Ole Floyd, I call every rattlesnake that, the whole lot.
He's curled up in his defensive stance; I better not
say stance as snakes don't stand; defensive spot.
So Barb and I sit; we'd stare him down; such rot.

What a lovely way to spend a fall afternoon.
Playing, I won't blink before you game, with a snake.
But then we're not your ordinary buffoon,
no sir, we love and admire our Floyd's, no mistake.

October 25, 2011

Two

Growing Older

I can't remember when I was young,
the feel of my body, the strength in my limbs.
How I sing now has not the range sung
when in high school choir; also my memory dims.

When I sit now for even a short duration,
getting up and standing causes pain in my back.
When I lost the flexibility during maturation
I couldn't say, but touching my toes, I seriously lack.

I could walk miles without the slightest pain,
and dance; I could twirl and dip with ease,
all night too if I felt like it; my partner fain.
As for intimacy prowess; in youth I could always please.

I ask myself, is there nothing I'm better at,
nothing I do now that has improved with age?
I can answer yes; for in gentleness I'll tip my hat,
and thoughtfulness too; I've become more sage.

October 27, 2011

Mystery No. 1

What do I look at every day,
sometimes white, often just tan,
often planted at dawn's first ray,
and usefulness not only to man?

A pair; most lucky are you,
but if single, perhaps a parking spot
near by where you're going to.
Co-mingling in a bar; you're doing what!

A three-point gain among lots of pain,
you'll need protection, that I'm sure.
But catch me outside and in the rain
you might be sorry for any exposure.

Take good care and you'll last for years,
but out in the sun you might get blistery.
Cats love them, but don't waste your tears
if you can't seem to answer this mystery.

October 27, 2011

In My Prime

In my prime with girls, I have lain;
Their wishes too, for there was never shame,
and certainly had there been, I'd take blame;
but given that none were made; I'd do it again.

In my prime I flew with the world's best,
those pilots that flew carrier jets out west.
Night and day, combat sorties not in jest,
but hitting targets with accuracy was the quest.

In my prime I'd hike through forest thick,
occasionally picking up the blood wood tick,
looking for lost hunters, and never getting sick
of the long, cold hours spent wading in swamps, ick!

In my prime I patrolled the highways,
looking for drug smugglers; long days.
At night for domestic disturbances it pays
to have back-up in case one has to taze.

In my prime I dreamed a lot too,
about how nice when I was through
being gung-ho, that I could begin to
relax, enjoy life as grandchild grew.

In my prime I planned my life
to include being with my wonderful wife,
not knowing that it would end in nonlife,
as she passed too quickly, like the stroke of a knife.

So now when I'm way past my prime
and I have plenty of idle time,
I do volunteer work, and in pastime
I write poetry, looking for words that rhyme.

October 27, 2011

A Shakespearean Proposal (in Modern English)

Sweet perfume; oh I smell its fragrance,
for it is everywhere that she has been.
It's in my hair, in my clothes, the luxe of romance.
I'm so dizzy I don't think I can count to ten.

And her hair, the nexus of the rainbow,
all colors perfectly wrapped into omneity.
To trace the spectrum, to find it now
is of little matter; I have known conspicuity.

Her laughter is the trill of singing angels,
it opens my ears, I catch its very timbre.
Remembering the tintinnabulation of hand bells,
I float, nay; I sail on in blissful rapture.

I cannot wait, she is vulnerable;
to seize this fortuity I must act now.
For to let salvation escape is unthinkable.
I will risk my life; this I fervently vow.

October 28, 2011

Omneity: the state of being all-comprehensive: allness

Fireflies in the Dark

I have this sense that something maybe wrong;
it's been gnawing at the back of my brain.
Not every day is it present; as in a throng
or when I'm driving to shop, or riding a train.

But at times when I'm alone and not distracted
I get this tic, like someone touched my neck.
The feeling leaves shortly thereafter, retracted
into me; where it goes, disappear to; I can't beck.

My doctor says it's just a random feeling,
nothing neurological; he's taken tests.
He further adds; this is common when I'm dealing
with older men; men that need their rests.

His placating attitude doesn't please me at all.
I thought about getting a second opinion;
it doesn't always work well; doctors eschew the call.
So that leaves me where I was before, society's minion.

Perhaps I'm thinking of fireflies in the dark.
I remember chasing them as a kid, along a lake;
I caught a few too; put them in a canning jar.
The next day they looked plain; no light did they make.

What this means to me is I'm like a firefly;
I have these moments when I light up too,
and then when I'm busy doing other things my
brains in daylight; I'm just an ordinary man with rue.

October 28, 2011

A Romanticist at Heart

I'm basically a romanticist at heart;
and I love opera, especially of Puccini's fame.
Tosca, Madama Butterfly, Turandot; all part
of my CD collection, and don't forget La Boheme.

The music of opera lives on; it seems forever.
And tenors in their magnificence, appear, effloresce
and then fade to quondam, for who ever
loves high C's will never forget in reminiscence.

Am I only a Puccini fan; I'll answer no.
Donizetti, Cilea, and don't forget Verdi;
they're my choices to name a few I know.
Its difficult buying classical CD's in a NM city.

I still have my LP record collection.
Some classic titles of complete operas LPs;
La Boheme with Pavarotti and Freni; I must mention
Domingo and Troyanos in Bizet's Carmen, I tease.

Of course there are the darker operas too,
those with only some romantic intrigue.
And German operas; Wagner and I'll name two;
Tannhäuser and Lohengrim; definitely top league.

But give me a romantic melody to lull sleep,
my favorite is Renée Fleming's "Haunted Heart".
While not opera entirely, Fleming will still keep
her title as opera's Diva; may she never depart.

October 29, 2011

Never

What a sad word that is;
never.

Did you tell me you loved me;
ever

You were always changing the subject;
clever.

Why did you always want control;
lever.

What you said on that last night;
over.

Is this then what you really want;
rover.

What a sad word that is;
forever.

October 29, 2011

If I Live to be a Hundred

If I live to be a hundred,
I surely
    Would be a rich man
    and give away millions.
    I'd be a dancing Dan
    with horrendous bunions.

If I live to be a hundred,
I wouldn't
    Want a cane
    unless like Fred Astaire
    and a pretty Jane
    I'd dance with flair.

If I live to be a hundred,
I shouldn't
    Want lots of wives
    I'm no King Faruk,
    and I'd stay out of dives
    and be a Chicago crook.

If I live to be a hundred,
I'd probably
    Take lots of pills
    to keep fit
    and have a loving cat
    I could pet a bit.

If I live to be a hundred,
I'd write
>   Poems in the thousands,
>   my fingers sore,
>   but I'd get garlands
>   and be famous in lore.

October 29, 2011

The Ratcheting of Guns

Do you hear the ratcheting of guns
They sound throughout our imperfect planet.
Trying to keep score; tallying loses and wons,
is a full-time job of a statistician and www.net.

It used to be that wars were fought for land,
but today's scrimmages are politically motivated.
Is it then right to sacrifice our young and
productive soldiers to stop massacres perpetuated

For everyone knows that both sides in battle
have their good and bad points pondered.
I therefore, in good faith, propose, with no tattle,
a David and Goliath fight; no money laundered.

Of course this simple solution won't be acceptable
to important countries like USA; it wouldn't take risk
of a ne'er-do-well country having a fighter cabal
that would field a "David"; totally unacceptable and brisk.

October 30, 2011

You Are No More

Oh my aching heart; to ease it I implore,
send me an amorous response most dear;
of tenderness and soothing words to explore,
for no more do they reach me to heal and restore.

Write of the times we spent walking,
stopping to watch Butterfly sip nectar
from bright, yellow flowers, gently waving.
Those moments I cherish; what I'm after.

At the bubbling stream where we dipped toes;
the water ice cold, little it mattered to our feet.
I took your hand and we crossed; no woes;
we were happy, the sun warm, in love, complete.

And then we parted; so sad the day.
You turned and gave a little wave;
I felt a tear and tried to wipe it away,
but you were gone; how hard to be brave.

Now in forlornity all I have is what lingers
of our last day together and my saddened heart.
Fondly, I caress your picture in my fingers;
you are no more...forever we will be apart.

October 31, 2011

The Lighthouse

The lighthouse is my guide,
said the trawler man to me.
It guides me past rocks outside
the harbor; it tells me where to be.

I remember, oh, a few years ago
there was a storm; nor'easter.
If it hadn't been for that lights glow
I wouldn't have made it back, no sir.

I left the bar, saying a farewell,
for on the morrow I flew back home.
The trawler man waved, I could tell
he had more to say; enough to call a tome.

I grabbed a postcard of that lighthouse
with the cottage windows brightly lit.
The keeper; was it a woman at the house
She kept her garden well; colors every bit.

At home I took time to write a poem
about the trawler man and his story.
I wondered if local fishermen were solemn
when they spotted the flash, not having to worry.

November 1, 2011

Tonight the Quail Came Home

Tonight the Quail came home, in force too.
I had wondered where they had gone, as
only a pair or two had been part of summer's zoo.
Maybe a hunter (out of season?); reasons I'll pass.

So I listened, and this is their story.
"So great to be back, I see your young grew,
mine were lost in storm, but second hatch, glory
what a bunch, kept me hunting for food new."

"Yes, we found that feed was plentiful
at ranch nearby; had to watch out for
feral cats though, they made our day eventful.
Saw my hubby pass by just now, has a leg sore."

"Hi, I'm the gal that had my nest next
to yours, and that storm was really bad, whew!
Kept my brood safe though; owner had axed
a tree and under it we waited; and you"

"We got caught out in the open grass area,
flooded my family, poor little ones couldn't
stand the wet and cold; just died and bury a
problem, so left them there, maybe I shouldn't"

"There's talk from the single males that
a Rattlesnake ate the eggs of three
nests; must have looked funny, what,
with little bumps in his slithering body be."

"Well at least the covey is back again,
we are very lucky to have such a nice
man to feed us twice each day, amen.
Heard his mate died; hey, soon there'll be ice."

November 2, 2011

Home of Forgotten Dreams

Sometimes I like to do what psychologist's
call "free thought" or "free thinking", and
use this exercise to write poems, least
I run out of ideas (fat chance) I've canned

I bet there are thousands of untold stories
that die each day with their holders
I'd like to ask Grandma Anna; what worries,
what love affairs, what she remembered of elders

Maybe a lot of seniors need that extra push,
that something that will spur them on
to write stories, poems, a diary or journal; hush
with secrets whispered to their pillows, anon

We're recording Native Indian stories, so
why not ask those over 60 to jot down
whatever they feel like; these journals to go
to their heirs of course, to do as they now own

I thought that since I at age 74 could
write poems at will; that then maybe
I could coax a few my age; would
they write poems too, or perhaps a diary

If nothing else, let all these recordings
be gathered and stored in a library
where smart young people; researching,
might find a trove of stories, so merry

And don't you say that this isn't my cup,
that writing is too hard; for I will
answer that you can voice record; yup,
that doesn't take talent; easy as paying a bill

This large library, building, whatever; I'd
call it the "Thompson Home of Unsaid
Stories", or maybe I would abide
with "Home of Forgotten Dreams", to be read

November 2, 2011

Night Creatures

I always wondered about night creatures,
those nocturnal animals that lurk around
my property, finding left over cracked corn; nurtures
of Quail, Dove, Rabbits, and small birds abound.

One must be of the Skunk, for occasionally
its noxious smell lingers at dawn's light.
Some Rabbits prefer night; I wonder why as certainly
the road kills escalate when they're about at night.

Small mammals too; Moles, Kangaroo Rats,
Field Mice and even Feral Cats come out
to feed and play; one mustn't forget the Bats.
Owls, the silent gliders eat rodents, no doubt.

But it's the bigger ones that perk my interest,
those four legged animals like Coyote and
Javelina (what some call Gregory Peccary), don't rest
until daylight and often are seen as a band.

I cannot in all honesty say what "thing"
plumps on my roof at night for it's never
seen by my eye; it's coming and going
to quick for observation; as much as I endeavor.

Cold blooded animals, like Floyd, our summers
Rattlesnake, Lizards, Toads, and I must not
forget night insects, all varieties in numbers
too large to count, are all present in my lot.

And on a windless summer night I might
hear the plaintful hoot, hoot of the Owl,
then a softer hoot, hoot, far off, out of sight
comes a mates answer to a loving call.

November 5, 2011

You Can Never

You can never take back;
A cutting remark
Your feelings in anger
A blemish or mark
Your cowardliness in danger

You can never make up;
Years spent in jail
That thank you never sent
A slacked jibe of a sail
An arrow that is bent

You can never redo;
A missed opportunity
A bad landing
A massacred community
The wrong branding

You can never duplicate;
Your first roller coaster ride
A near miss
A child's toothless smile wide
Your first kiss

November 5, 2011

He Sang a Poignant Ballad

His voice, although lacking in lung capacity,
gives a pleasing tremolo and resonates well
with the more senior members of this city
Perhaps they suspect in age there's beauty; they can tell

He sang a poignant ballad, dedicated
to his departed wife, titled; "The Girl That I Marry"
Tears might be seen as the words demonstrated
his clear devotion, his suffering, his loss to carry

Music maybe the perfect medium to express loss,
for those receptive to melody may on the morrow
remember fondly those ballads sung to remain
in their sub consciousness, to be balm for any sorrow

I say then, sing on you Apollo for all your worth,
let the muse Euterpe guide you in time,
for your gift is to gladden dolente hearts, bring forth
joyousness through singing melodies in rhyme

November 6, 2011

When We Will Meet Again

I've wondered about when we will
meet again; there doesn't seem
to be any reason for not agreeing; still
this step requires your input which I esteem

Thanksgiving and Christmas are family fare,
so I had thought about celebrating the end
of 2011 and the start of 2012 together, but are
we ready for this short of notice I send

When I think about airport weather delays,
difficulty in driving, and mid-winter blues,
I think a jaunt to warmer climes plays
much better than slushy snow and overshoes

You had mentioned your school age neighbor
asking you to go south, I don't remember where,
but perhaps I could join; there being no other
alternative that I can think of or dare

If this even sounds plausible, then I
think that we can broach this topic
when we talk again, for poems may try
to bargain ideas, but fail in nitty-gritty logic

November 7, 2011

Don't Buy China Items

I've heard it twice now; buy American made
Especially, don't purchase items made in China
But do these people understand their plan laid,
for serious repercussions will happen; not kinda

Say this becomes a national cause, not unlike
the "Occupy Wall Street" type movement;
what might be the consequences, could you buy a bike,
play your X-Box, or dine on china (no pun meant)

Take a "big box" store like Wal-Mart for example,
but any armed forces exchange or Bx is the same;
outside of food items, almost everything ample
is from China, Japan, Korea, India, Mexico, you name

Buy a television; there are no "Made in USA"
TV's you could buy; so you opt for music listening
and all radios, CD players, and spare parts say
made in "Not USA"; you're not doing well on winning

Sure you can buy US automobiles; I do, but
even Ford, GM, and Chrysler use parts from
Mexico and Canada, so even then if you cut
out the Japanese and German autos, you look dumb

No. and I say confidently, this is serious,
but not buying foreign items is much like
cutting off your nose to spite your face; curious,
the way we succeed is to buy, buy, and buy a bike

November 8, 2011

The Art of Feeding a Cat

Unfortunately, there are too many people
that have not fully mastered; oh woe!;
the art of feeding a cat; such staple
how-to-do books abound in libraries, so go!

In the meantime, let me offer this advice;
first, that cats do not abide by human time,
that is, their meal time does not always dice
with ours, so be prepared, don't whine

When you do feed your feline, no amount
of food is ever accepted as *fait accompli*
The cat will eat what it wants, but count
yourself lucky that she leaves quietly to pee

You're feeling confident, the cat has been fed,
so you relax with coffee and morning paper
A yowl, loud enough to wake up the dead;
you frantically seek out the sound maker

How is it possible that little cuddlesome cat
has made what you'd expect from a lion
or a tiger; a noise of ear splitting dB at
or near your pain level; you ask; is he dy'in

No he isn't about to leave his berth,
he is not satisfied, plain and simple
You check his food, its empty; how on earth
Did you put out enough, surely it was ample

Cats do not communicate on our plane,
they are like aliens and we know zip
The yowl might mean her tummy hurts; plain
enough to the average bloke, but me, I'm hip

To talk cat you need to understand; one,
they're always hungry, and two, they're always
hungry; you understand that bit of dumb
logic and you're home free; so get a dog, it pays

November 9, 2011

A Lasting Poem

By now you've gone through about twenty
or so poems and if your eyes are still open,
then this last one is such a relief, it's plenty!
Perhaps then, you'll halve them next time, you ken?

To make your job easier I'll pen a poem,
a poem of love, for surely its needed now.
I have entrusted my soul *intra vitam*
with my poetry because I fully trust thou.

I believe there are different forms fair
love can take; we both then have known
the first love that will always be there;
the other is the fair love that we now own.

Then through our notes, our lengthy calls,
and yes, my poetry, we will foster this
close relationship to last forever, there be no balks.
This is true love, I affirm and gladly seal with a kiss.

So here then is a poem to gladden your heart,
a poem to caress and wear around your neck,
a locket given most fair, there to never part,
but to always remind that I'm yours to beck.

November 9, 2011

Angry Old Man

Am I an angry old man,
one who pooh-poohs one and all,
the ideas of those genius's who can
invent the social network call

Probably not, for I'm not angry,
however, I am an older member,
who laments life's trials; we augury
I also feel the current is building; remember

I have this theory on the personification
of the angry old man; it allows those
who write stories to have hoodoo dollification;
those that can be blamed; get the bloody nose

But in truth, angry old men, finally
have reached the point where their comments can't
possibly hurt them; for Soc. Security and its ally,
Medicare renders them sufficient, so they rant

November 10, 2011

Happy Old Men

Because of the liberals clamoring
for equal media treatment, I have
decided to voice my supporting
philodoxical views on old men's rave

Most old men, I'm told, live life
according to their spouses desires;
which means they don't use a knife
to popular senior events such as bazaars

In fact, it has been said, old men
are quite gentle creatures seeking
out furry companions which are often
slovenly dogs that do outdoors leaking

I add what church choirs purport;
their being about 90% female, I attest,
old men are joyful singers giving support
in the bass range; being noisy when at rest

There are also, and I stress, very few
that imbibe, usually at various fraternal
gatherings, sporting activities, and when due
to what is referred as inherited paternal

November 11, 2011

Cycle of Life

Leaves aswirl around me
falling softly, dead
spent of summers
energy to be transformed

I walk and remember
youthful days
no thoughts of dying
seeking love

The leaves are still falling
am I too
to lie among those
of spent vitality

Come spring, fresh and new
flowers, the early
ones with tiny
blossoms

A child calls out
mommy watch me
see the pretty
tree buds

November 12, 2011

Feeling Safe

Do you feel safe beside me,
I asked, not really seeking
an answer, just letting it be
said; my thoughts of love leaking

Her smile, as she turned towards,
gave me all the answer I needed
She mouthed familiar words; rewards
I placed for safe keeping; ceded

And then with a hop, skip and run
she charged ahead, her ponytail flowing,
asking me to watch her fun,
seeing if I feel safe with her going

At the top of the rise she stood watching,
was I coming? Oh don't be such a waif,
you love me I know, but catching
me is my answer to feeling safe

November 12, 2011

So Lonely Is Despair

I tried to compose a love ballad
    but my heart was elsewhere
Try as I might I could not get my
    pen to even write a simple prayer

What sort of malaise is effecting
    my heart and my strength
It must be very strong as I
    battle it now at length

Is there no antidote that can
    cure this cursed affliction,
for without the elixir I will die
    and never taste of your affection

So lonely is despair when I'm in love;
    when the goal seems unobtainable
If I could only receive your
    promise, then I might recover all

On the wings of an Eagle comes my
    heartache reprieve
It is sent from you, the Eagle says,
    to save me, not to bereave

Then at last I can write my ballad
    of overflowing love to you,
knowing that within your receptive heart
    it will be read as being true

November 12, 2011

Loss of Energy

I asked the question at Sunday's meeting
of poets; do you feel a loss of energy
after writing some poems, because I'm feeling
run down and very tired; no vivacity

One answered that with him, if the subject
of the poem wasn't frivolity, then he too felt
a sort of loss, but he wondered if the object
written about might contribute to the welt

I replied that I hadn't felt any blows
to my body yet, but perhaps the simile
was apt, as it could represent the flows
of my energy; like romantic sorrow of dear Emily

When this feeling is more acute I find
that I have written poems that are dark
By that I mean, soul searching my mind,
seeking out the reasons for or against; no lark

If I find that a poem is hard to rhyme,
or that I search long for words that portend
my feelings within me, then perhaps I'm
focusing too hard; the subject matter must end

Whither this puissance loss comes now,
after this poem is finished I will not say
I can't, like with a faucet, vacillate how
and when it happens; there just is no way

November 13, 2011

A Word

Often a word
Spoken felt warming
The heart of accord
Is all that's needed

Over distance a bay
Answered cogent too
Bona fide and lay
Amongst baneful dolor

Mindful nascent course
Apollo answers yes
For cunctation forgotten
Solivagant and dauntless

November 14, 2011

A Word (translated)

Often a word
That is spoken is felt warming
The heart of an agreement
And that's all that's needed

Over distance a shout
is heard and answered convincingly too
In honesty as it lays
Among the hurt and sorrow

Mindful of a new course
The poet answers yes
For being wavering is forgotten
So rambling onward with courageous resolution

November 14, 2011

How Does Love Die

Tell me then, how does love die,
does it end in a stall-spin spiral
Not recoverable, the end inevitably lie,
or with corrections become survival

I've seen many love trysts end,
not pretty and sometimes violent
There appears that for parties to bend,
one must accept status quo or be silent

But silence in love is a no starter
for building up hatred persists
until again it causes love to faulter;
no longer a successful ending exists

The cause for this love to be dying
needs to be found and quickly;
for once, look at the beginning
as love was present, obviously

Then what enabled it to sour,
to move from adoring to boring
Did it begin small and then roar
to fighting; was it constant warring

At this root cause we must act
to roll-back feelings is difficult;
but if both acknowledge the fact,
then counseling may work it out

November 17, 2011

Twixt Two Settings

Am I twixt two settings
One to remain in memory awe
The other, in love a new, rendering
Love fervently, boundless, in raw

To mediate these endings now
Require sage of the thoughtful
An oracle of wisdom, but how
Is this no-man's landful

For either ending causes woe
In transit I'll decide, divide
What loyalties, what emotions pose
The end, my decision, I'll abide

November 17, 2011

I'm Having Fright

I've written lately poems of betrayal;
fictitious poems of love misused
Am I toying, giving hints; if so, they pale
compared to real life tales if perused

Who knows what unconscious thought
spill out in poems written so freely
I try to know the direction I have brought
but sometimes I wonder, did I know, really

Am I a twixt as a previous poem explores
I'm having a difficult time getting insight,
where I am (my real me) from the scores
of poems written on love; I'm having fright

November 19, 2011

My Repose

At one side, music protean, archived
So varied, nobility, bourgeois, to rabble
Although many might invert the babble
These jeweled, compacted disks survived
Unleashing romance, treachery, humor
And some of all; story told in song
With flourish and crescendo the throng
Sometimes hidden behind books, the rumor

In the middle, technology supreme
Gleefully, hoots and whistles, if not muted
Greets you by name, no shame, not denuded
The pling pling, buzz buzz, all the cream
Of young, effulgent minds alchemistical
My work transposed, tantivy into presentability
Always storing, library like the enormity
But watch out, *anguis in herba*, gist inimical

On the other side visual somnolence
Among gaiety, romance and history
Poirot, Wolfe, and Midsomer mystery
Aeonic viewing, for divergence
Besides hang transfigurations
Replaced by seasonal conditions
Providing multiple image renditions
Clandestine vestiges, inspirations

And at the head, the oeillade
Photomontage fills the wall
Memories of ago, familiar all
Indoors captures, alas, none of glade
At reach accoutrements of life
No nostrum remedy, but hopefully
Aids for ails, taken regularly
And by *viet armis*, to counter strife

November 21, 2011

Did it Rain Today

Did it rain today
Was the pitter-patter
My heart at play
Tell me, I'm a dither

Was that a knock
Go, check the door
It wasn't the clock
Striking the hour

I dreamt of you
In black and white
Fading, lingering as dew
Perhaps it was night

The mail came at two
A bill, subscription lapse
I checked again too
Empty, tomorrow perhaps

Come, eat your meal
You need the energy
Say, I'll make a deal
Finish, I'll call the clergy

I won't accept she's gone
Answer the phone
Hello, I'm finished, done
Yes, he's here alone

November 21, 2011

I Take So Much Joy

I take so much joy
Watching her clean
The fur damp, boy
Your hairs a sheen

Your eyes are closed
Is licking fur tasty
Are cats then transposed
As Elves in ecstasy

Curling up, back to me
Safe, contentment, you mew
In sleep, dreaming, lazily
Remembering dinner too

Save these fond moments
Feel your own repose
For the time portents
An empty bed expose

November 21, 2011

The Feeling Deeds

That last line sent shivers all over,
does it take my mood to be in sync,
or do words alone create this feeling; never
mind, I'm talking to myself, seeking that link

Maybe it's the flow, the way I put it down;
a cadence or rhythm, some secret coding,
and when it's written, the prickling began grow 'in
I can read it later and the same effect exploding

An it's not every poem that is sad
that I get the urge to cry a tear,
so maybe I'm on to something, dad;
certainly this poem raises no rupture

Let's stop right here lad, you're wrong,
you shouldn't write to make this appear;
that's dishonest, the affect comes along
after you write a line, a stanza, you hear

So, pen your lines of love long lost;
if the message is clear and it 'reads',
then if you get that 'certain' feeling post,
well, you've got a bonus, the feeling deeds

November 21, 2011

You Can't be Mean and Be A Poet

You can't be mean and be a poet,
it's not in their genes and personality
Poets are a happy-go-lucky conglomerate
of sex, age, moral persuasion, nationality

Poetry is like taking a taxi ride;
while a novel is taking an ocean liner
traveling between two continents; wide
Book authors are despicable whiners

You can memorize poems you love,
but try memorizing "Gone with the Wind"
Poets don't smoke; but as for loving, they rove,
but not in anger, so sir; kiss and be kind

If you plan on being a mean person;
tell it verbally or write a short note
If you tried poetry, the original reason
for hate will be lost in the stanzas wrote

November 22, 2011

Frayed Cuffs

I glanced briefly at my resting feet;
saw frayed cuffs on my trousers,
and wondered why the rest was neat;
did it depend upon who were users

Since I don't wear dress shirts much
I'm not concerned about frayed collars
So I got thinking about other things, such
as kitchen towels, throw rugs, and dollars

We're a throw-away society I guess;
look at cell phones, jam and pickle jars,
and socks; why, who ever darns, unless
you're a soldier, like in WWII wars

Is it the same way with our elders;
are they forgotten or discarded at age;
can you mend the tears that glitters
in grandma's eyes when she's in dotage

I wrote a poem. "Home of Forgotten Dreams",
it spoke of the dream never posted
Perhaps these are the frays of life's seams;
the patched lives waiting to unravel; wasted

Whenever I see a young person's dress
with designer frays and old patches;
their believing what's chic and modish,
I remember an old man; he sits and watches

November 24, 2011

Three

They Write to Cross Swords

I've been reading American poets
    and I'm rather confused
It would seem to me, a simple man,
    that one might understand
what a poem is about when reading
    the stanzas I perused
So many mid-twentieth century scholarly
    poets are abstruse as they stand

Now, occasionally I too pen a poem
    with unfamiliar words
but the gist of the poem is easy
    to decipher, to explain
But maybe I've got this all wrong;
    they write to cross swords
with other academic poets; sort of
    one-upmanship; a rivalrous game

November 25, 2011

The Fallow of My Life

I'm in the fallow of my life,
not used up, but just laying idle
A long time married; now no wife,
maybe I should up and skedaddle

But what would happen to Twinkie
and my dear friend up north
I just can't leave here, give a winkie,
say I'll be back soon; going forth

No, for being in fallow, I can renew,
be useful, productive again, I'm sure
Just because Uncle Sam pays well too,
I can't just lay here, parous and pure

Plant me in the spring, I'm now able
I'll germinate and grow in abundance;
a bumper crop to harvest; and in the fable,
to write poetry that nourishes existence

November 25, 2011

Worth Some Exaggeration

At days ending, I think of you
Sweeping my cobwebs for the view
And clearer now I have no cause
Delaying my sight or to pause

I capture your face in memory
Saving it for a poem story
About love and trust from afar
Throwing in moonbeams and a star

People always ask why, to me,
Are poems writ in hyperbole
I answer, lovers celebration
Is worth some exaggeration

December 7, 2011

The Inner Me

The inner me sometime roams free
when I'm resting listening to melodies
that enrapture and captivate me;
I know not where it goes or what it remedies

For I have awaken to find a poem new,
penned by me, yet unknownst in memory
I marvel at the potency of lines drew,
wondering if they were stored in some armory

I know that deep, deep within my very soul
lay reams of poetic thought waiting patiently;
praying that I in repose unleash inner me to dole
another poem of unremitted love, given freely

Or, perhaps when drowsiness awakens and stirs,
my mind still foggy from sleep profoundable,
a poem is given in tenderness, sweetly purrs
that impels the heart in ways imponderable

November 25, 2011

A World Below

I noticed her belly
Swollen beneath covers
Not rain in deep gully
Could cheat these two mateloters
To part lovers

Upon that smallish bed
Above the floor below
My fondle soon then led
Is it alright you should know
Yes likely so

And with our unheard cries
We slept snuggled a top
Least falls to floor and lies
Yet even that cannot stop
Our navies SOP

Little did he then know
That in her warm embrace
A child in time would grow
To be born with he in place
A world below

November 27, 2011

It Came With the Rain and Wind Last Night

It came with the rain and wind last night
I might have noticed, had I not been so busy
It settled in, found a nice warm spot right
Outside my bedroom door; waiting there easy

Around midnight or so, I fell asleep finally
The cat was fidgety; getting up, then turning around
Then she was silent too; soft purrs eventually
It too waited; only the rain and wind making sound

The next morning the sun shone through the bower
Awakening small birds; their chirping done fervently
The telephone rang and rang; there was no answer
I was sound asleep; Twinkie at my feet; quiescently

November 25, 2011

She Moves Oh So Slowly

She moves oh so slowly
Her face always to the sky
No birds for they've all flown away
And where could they have built a nest

The sound a deep rumble nearing where
Mountain men try to halt her
Alas she conquers all
Moving on and on relentlessly

Wrinkled now with age millenniums
Would scar any whitened face
Then in a forested glen she stops
And starts crying with hug sobs

Her life is ending but oh so glorious
The gods if available probably clapped
They sang a song in her passing
Come back little birds come mating

November 27, 2011

The Pat, Pat, Pat

I'll have to investigate I told Twinkle
Both of us had heard the pat, pat, pat
On the metal roof; more than just a tinkle
I'll bet I know, I said, it's that Pack Rat

I don't know, said Twinkle, it could be a cat
Maybe that black tom looking for mice
You could be right, but if so, tell that drat
Flea battened cat that catching the mouse is nice

So next morning I got the ladder ready
Climbed up and surveyed the roof at all
Walking in places was slippery, not steady
But I could see tracks, they were quite small

I followed them at roof edge to a Pine tree
Which grew thirty or more feet above the ground
Upon a branch, almost hidden, but I could see
What had made the pat, pat, pat was found

So Twinkle we both made faulty postulation
Although we were close, but get no dimes
It was a Squirrel, I saw his final destination
He's after pine cones which fall from our Pines

November 27, 2011

A Simple Poem

Here is a simple poem for you to follow
Simple English words; foreign words I won't allow
Mostly it will be snappy
The kind to make you happy
So if you feel the urge, go ahead and bellow

When winter sends you its first dusting
Panic; where's my chains; Oh, but they're rusting
But with 4-wheel drive
Or even front-wheel drive
You can forget chains; you won't be cussing

Then in later weeks, when the blizzard hits
You'll say, shucks man, these are just little bits
Of snow and any fool will drive
But watch out, he might not survive
Cause I'm coming out; going to the Ritz

Then in spring, that's June in snowman land
The flooding starts and they're spreading sand
So staying a jump ahead
For you'll always dread
The freezing rain, and they're out of melting sand

And while all this is happening to you
In my land south we got a few inches too
But it melted by noon
And that wasn't too soon
Because I had planting of flowers and scrubs to do

November 28, 2011

Go Rest, Congeal

When I looked in, the room was empty
Of all the fun, the gayety, the serendipity
Everything had been stripped; it was bare
Awaiting the new owner, a man so debonair
These walls will never reveal
Anything at all, go rest, congeal

So many owners, I've lost my count
And adding them up, enormous the amount
Waxing the floors, new paint, never peel
So he advertised, dancing a jig or perhaps a reel
These walls will never reveal
Anything at all, go rest, congeal

The beginning, scarcity of lumber, the war
Taking everything; Napoleon saying *c'est la guerre*
But it was built, and finely too all the rooms
And they danced and danced, unaware that death looms
These walls will never reveal
Anything at all, go rest, congeal

November 29, 2011

Reaching a Turning

We are reaching a turning
Our relationship ending
Not a bang, but a whimper
A mewl with ardent fervor
Slowly the impassionate soul winds down
Till but a trickle remains, barely shown

Twas I the arrow did sling
Ah, but such rapture did bring
And poems flew mightily forth
To a friend, a love up north
So we haven't really lost, we're still friends
With memories that never really ends

So stay our weekly repartee
Born more in poems; speak freely
Often take reins of free thought
Nor reality has entirely brought
Of this I take the blame; not withstanding
For I've gained so much in understanding

Seek a missive now and then
For never the gods would end
This mellifluous content
This guilelessness to be sent
For if ever my mugient voice shall cease
I ask only for me to lie in peace

December 1, 2011

Free Falling

You have made a big mistake
Cutting off your lover mate
It's suicide; free falling
Without a parachute; mauling
You didn't have to do all this you know
Leave her be, let her make the first move now

What was wrong; the arrangement;
You set up the agreement
Did you get cold feet mister,
Afraid to love again her
She'll take it hard, you painted her corner
But that's par for you; always the loner

If there's a way out, tell me
If you say no; leave me be
I can survive the fallout
Telling you now there's no doubt
Stay; before you leave, if there's any chance
You know, could we still make it, the next dance

December 2, 2011

Rescue Me

Has my heart ceased its beating
I feel my life finishing
A body empty of love
Sinking, no help from above
My soul tormented, the heat intensifies
As in hell, my life in punishment dies

For I have misjudged her so
A nightingale to help me grow
No greater fool is one
Who attempts self heal as done
For deprivation of caring leads to
Endless self doubt, punishment that you'll rue

So I cry to rescue me
My hearts broken, I need thee
To love me, not as a friend
But forever, as your intend
In return I pledge an open mind here
To understand your needs, your wants dear

December 2, 2011

A Bad Arrow I Aver

Can I ever take it back
It was sent and not with tact
You'll get the package Monday
I explain it this Sunday
I'm writing many things I do not mean
Sending you everything, better not seen

Can I ever take it back
Would you forgive any lack
Of my judgment I ask you
I'll explain my feeling too
I was being melodramatic I implore
Trying new scenarios to explore

Some misguided idea
Insanity must I plea
I imagined your reply
My answer, I must then fly
To be next to you; fade to the sunset
Riding together; music to onset

Can you then forgive this fool
For trying, exploring each tool
Poets have in their quiver
A bad arrow I aver
And in time I'll make otherwise inane gaffs
Which in all sincerity should garner some laffs

December 3, 2011

Knowing Your Cat

She sits there watching me now
Contemplating I suppose
What I'm thinking; does it show
Indisputable; she goes
How did she figure out my staying put
Was it my relaxing, my shoeless foot

She's back again on my bed
Crouching with tail wrapped around
Signifying, I'm not fed
I'm not impressed, showing frown
I'll sit here writing poetry forever
Sure enough, she's surrendered in slumber

Knowing your cat is a plus
It takes time to understand
The difference between a fuss
And what's an in your face stand
For you never want to be in a fight
With someone who excels in war at night

December 4, 2011

Why A Title

Why a title for a poem
It's not exactly a tome
Is it for understanding
The gist, the story ending
Not always for sometimes a title hooks
You know, gets your glance; like racy books

But sometimes it's the ending
A key word or phrase lending
A link to the poets mind
What he or she wants to grind
I've used titles of one word many times
But more often it's a phrase which defines

To give you an example
Suppose 'His Quick Mind Doth Mull'
Is the title; you might think
A decision at the brink
Of course it could also be the poets
Liking of that phrase, a quirk which just fits

For myself I see titles
That gives a reader vitals
A hands up on the design
What the poet had in mind
We can't use a suggestive photo shot
Like novels; we use titles that are hot

December 4, 2011

New Mexico Snows

A comfy home is hard to beat
Walking around in stocking feet
And with the wind howling outside
Give thanks for heater warmth inside

The web reports Interstates close
Trouble too with pipes being froze
Below freezing all tomorrow
Without water neighbors borrow

Truckers camp out in cities near
Most have sleepers; pizza and beer
Law enforcement racks up overtime
Going to accidents and crime

TwinkleToes and I stay at home
We know better than to go roam
For one less vehicle on road
Helps the State road maintenance load

New Mexico snows give everyone
A chance to stop; see what's been done
Before going out in the snow
For icy roads may require tow

You can afford one day to rest
Your loved ones will say it's the best
Not risking your life for a day
When all you had to do was stay

December 5, 2011

The Stork

Now I ask you sir, is the Stork upside down
Or the contrary; is the Stork downside up
For you see sir, in all honesty I'm prone
To be inverse when not perverse with mix-up

I'm a person with ambidexterity
A rather rare accomplishment I'm lent
Which allows me to see ambiguity
Most of the time, otherwise I'm ambivalent

And if perchance I'm the latter, then the Storks
Position to itself is of no concern
But on the other hand, which is the same; works
To my advantage; ambivalence you learn

December 5, 2011

I Will Champion Loving

I'm told that with love comes grief
That this is true I've no doubt
For balance provides relief
As does winning confect rout

Should one then shun attachment
For surely happiness weighs
Sadness in the same ostent
As Romeo and Juliet stays

But we are also taught sweet
And bitterness complement
And who would refuse a treat
Knowing there must be payment

I will champion loving
Even if there is a cost
As I value ones sharing
Passion over being lost

December 5, 2011

Explaining Death of Grandma to a Child

Did you not know that Grandma died
For surely I would not have lied
And had I the power incarnate
She would live, sparing consolate

We live amid of lives asunder
A smile from one; frown from another
The daily ups and downs remind
That we enjoy life as we find

There's symmetry in everyday life
Sampling of happiness and strife
Had not sour would we enjoy sweet
Or silence antonymic tweet

So too in war there is balance
As friend and foe join alliance
Were this not so, would not chaos
Reign supreme, ever being loss

In ones marriage deep love amass
That in time it too takes a pass
In our birth there is also death
That we exhale and take in breath

If God determined a debit
Offsetting every births credit
Perhaps God had need of Grandma
To balance your birth for papa

December 6, 2011

Patterns

Patterns are interesting
Close your eyes, do you see them
Just sit still, are you resting
Quiet in your cubiculum

There, they appear intricate
Perhaps a little obscure
You can always speculate
I see red and black for sure

Small cuneiform shapes in red
With the black lines enclosing
My own Sistine overhead
Or just my blood transuding

When I speak of patterns here
I mean those of concreta,
Not *modus operandi* ware,
Escher's art work, et cetera

The patterns that intrigue me
Are natures by ownership
The veined leaf of an Elm tree
Or lake waves from tip to tip

Don't look too hard, miniscule
Will only frustrate your search
The same with measuring scale
The infinitum of inch

Resting peacefully are you,
Devoid your mind, drifting off
You'll be lucky seeing blue
Colored paint squares, but don't scoff

December 7, 2011

Memories, the Opium of Old Men

Memories, the opium of old men
Tales they tell over and over again
You know when this is happening to them
They sit with eyes closed, a smile or a grin

I can vouch that this is true, mark my words
As I relate memories of long ago
To set the stage; my early teen accords,
The years following the great world war two

A small town in southern Minnesota
I'm exploring along the gravel road
Which runs from my home; I've no iota
What I'm planning to do, so don't you goad

Passing the School for the Deaf; mom works there
No one outside, its summer time; schools out
A Chrysler station wagon passes near
Golfers I gather from their ruckus shout

They want me to caddy; no way buddy
I did that last year, paid only a dime
Had to clean his clubs too, they were muddy
I'll pass this one up, there isn't much time

I'm passing the military school; clock chimes
Used to wake me at night; ding, dong, ding, dong
It meant quarter past and many the time
I lay awake waiting for the next bong

The golfers wave to me, they're happy lot
I wave back, doesn't hurt to be friendly
Now there's woods on both sides, sweet smell of rot
A dead hare, run over accidentally

I look at it closely, I have no knife
I could have used a good luck Rabbit's foot
Wondering what happened to take its life
A friend says God cries, I wonder, thought moot

I've reached my destination; a gully
From the culver a trickle of water
A path leading down, steep, my hands sully
A snake weaves by quickly, it's a Garter

I hear birds but can't see any, I wonder
If this is a refuge for them also
The gully widens, don't want to blunder
Dad says there's hobo camp by where trains go

At the tracks by Fourteenth Street there's a train
The Rock Island chugs by, I give some waves
White bellowing puffs of steam amid soot rain
It thunders north, the caboose flag caves

And then silence as I walk the tracks back
Keeping a watchful eye for any hobos
The Straight River isn't straight; why, I lack,
Any answer leaves my mind, ask Faribos

Fleckenstein's Brewing giant beer bottle
On my left as I'm taking the road by
I see dad's Dodge car, better not dawdle
Taking the path to the Deaf School, I fly

Past the steam plant, Mr. Dwyer works there
I like the campus, lots of trees and lop
Brother Dick and I practice football here
I'm home again, mom can I have a pop

December 9, 2011

Gooseberries

As a youngster exploring Shumway street
It was paved only to top of the hill
From there on north it was gravel; concrete
Was never considered; who'd pay the bill

I've written about this road before too
But this time I'm not exploring gullies
Just past the golf course an open meadow
There along a fence were the Gooseberries

Most of the summer they were prickly tart
And biting them caused you to pucker up
But if baked with sugar as a dessert
Or made into jam they were like syrup

One day, maybe I was in tenth grade then
Four girls walked by my house, not unheard of,
Asking if I knew where they might happen
To find Gooseberries; these girls I knew, no love

I said hi and yes I knew where some were
One brunette, her parents and mine were friends
Said, why don't you come along, show us where
Having nothing better to do, amends

I took them to the spot where I had been
The girls, with pails, started picking berries
I said that in the meadow more were seen
So oft they went, laughing, girls are sillies

What I hadn't said, well they never asked
Was that cows were in the meadow feeding
Soon yells I heard and four girls ran, not basked,
Towards me and the fence, the cows were beating

I yelled back to them, stop your running now
The cows resumed feeding; girls rejected
They had lost their Gooseberry pails in the row
Staring at me, I knew no thanks expected

December 10, 2011

Random Thoughts

It's enchantment time, wow
I'm settled, open to
Random thoughts, where fore now
Are they present, waiting too
Or, ambush rue

For if they do waylay
Sorrow is not wealthy
Where then the ransom pay
The alternate not healthy
Be I stealthy

A filter of thoughts sought
Countering defenses
Can they even be bought
Does any of this make sense
Perhaps nonsense

Let me restart; begin
Accepting vetted thoughts
Satisfaction certain
My mind at rest, no more naughts
Just silly jots

December 11, 2011

A Grandeur Christmas Gift

One wonders where all of this leads
It's like driving at night without lights
For certainly a surprise deeds
Folly unforeseeable last rites

Turning on all lights, I present
A poem of ponderable amour
Openly stated, your way sent
To dispose those glums away, I'm sure

I give this gift to you freely
Absolved of tare, there's no postage due
I've planned the date most carefully
For arrival by Christmas day too

And in return an open heart
No less, no more will satisfy me
Having you always be a part
Is a grandeur Christmas gift from thee

December 11, 2011

A Sinuosity

The trailing of a snake

A Snails' viscosity

A young boys' summer rake

A Sailing odyssey

An Ocean swimming Hake

Weaving traffic in city

The waves upon a lake

Curvilinearity

Curve fitting data bank

An electrical AC

A hair curler mistake

Curvaceous entity

What lost hunters tracks take

Periodicity

December 12, 2011

Dark Haunting Eyes

She has those dark haunting eyes
Deep pools, the unfathomable
They are asking of me, whys
Answers for, I'm not capable
Or escapable

I'm not sure I should even try
She sees through all of my lies
Dumbfounded, bewildered I,
For to apologize implies
My having *faiblesse*

Perhaps in another locale
When her moods in penitence
Trying again to channel
Good points, even as reticence
Bespeaks innocence

December 12, 2011

They Become the Salve

Have you ever observed a cat preening
They do it in the open, no screening
Although they seem to bite, it's only fur
and positions; good acrobats mirror

Then it is curl up and nap time again
Settling in the same spot she began
The reason I think cats need to wash up
With sleeping, they allow dirt to buildup

But kidding aside, cats deserve credit
They are perhaps too clean; there I've said it
We hold them on our laps, kiss their noses
It's really no worse than kissing roses

For their toilet they are methodical
Forget to clean, they become radical
Leave their pile in places unexpected
So make sure each day, have it collected

Cats are wonderful companions to have
Have a hurting heart, they become the salve
They will keep a part of you warm when cold
Just feed them four times a day, they won't scold

December 12, 2011

Poems From The Womb

In spaces small he feels secure
Cubby holes, churches were used
Hiding souls that sought them harm
He feels no threat, yet
It is where comfort comes again

Like prisons, a cell was all
Reaching walls opposite laying down
His nichus
His stateroom and airplane cockpit
Small, confined, no danger

After She died
Traded cell for small bedroom, shuns
Large master bed, cramming all his wants
In blissful recollection he pens
Poems from the womb

December 13, 2011

Affaire d'amours

I hear the sound of your heart beating
Even when I'm so far distantly
It's like a soft drum beat I'm meeting
Marching slowly inexplicably

I hear the words you'd whisper asleep
Those secret, held in your heart, murmurs
Telling of undying love so deep
These thoughts I cherish as *affaire d'amours*

I see your image when day dreaming
You appear demurely, but a smile
Breaks out as you see me too, beaming
And then we embrace, a kiss ethereal

I feel your warm hand on my shoulder
As I pause, waiting for my ride home
Telling me you are with me forever
And I know I'll make it through, alone

December 15, 2011

Something More Mellow

I need to write something more mellow
My poems are darkening once again
Perhaps something you'd want to bellow
To cry out in joy, but with no pain

I'll write of love that will be a change
But I'll be careful as love can turn sour
How about a teen romance from the range
Cowboys are quiet, bashful, want more

Picture this, pig-tailed lass in jeans
Her cowboy fella with wide brimmed hat
Meeting at the county barn, he leans
To give her a kiss, his buddies all clap

A sailor in love; always good copy
Swashbuckling with bell bottomed trousers
But watch the ale, he might get sloppy
Kiss him, but remember they're rousters

A sailor might bring a valentine
Made with seashells, colorful for you
But careful, he might be spending time
In another port where he's someone's beau

But if mellowness is important
I would suggest you visit the first
Nursing home for well-aged, compliant
Men who will play whist, they're not the worst

December 16, 2011

Something More Mellow

I need to write something more mellow
My poems are darkening once again
Perhaps something you'd want to bellow
To cry out in joy, but with no pain

I'll write of love that will be a change
But I'll be careful as love can turn sour
How about a teen romance from the range
Cowboys are quiet, bashful, want more

Picture this, pig-tailed lass in jeans
Her cowboy fella with wide brimmed hat
Meeting at the county barn, he leans
To give her a kiss, his buddies all clap

A sailor in love; always good copy
Swashbuckling with bell bottomed trousers
But watch the ale, he might get sloppy
Kiss him, but remember they're rousters

A sailor might bring a valentine
Made with seashells, colorful for you
But careful, he might be spending time
In another port where he's someone's beau

But if mellowness is important
I would suggest you visit the first
Nursing home for well-aged, compliant
Men who will play whist, they're not the worst

December 16, 2011

All Multiphasics

What I haven't written about
Well, there is mathematics
And sea shells and sheriff clout
Then there's flying aerodynamics
All multiphasics

Teaching college students well
My credo at Northwestern
Chapman, La Verne; show and tell
And last, Western New Mexico's turn
Math, they want to learn

Cones, cowries, volutes and Cassis
All in Latin like *noblis*
That's a species of *Conus*
This is business, no beach shells in this
Malacologists

Sheriff Deputy, the best
Counties elected office
All certified by test
Just like the law enforcement police
Friendly and very nice

Flew Navy single seat jets
Off aircraft carriers too
Vietnam combat sorties vets
Retired then commercial airplanes flew
Patriot true blue

A hospital manager
Psychiatric emotion
Adolescents, long termers
Setup and ran organization
Administration

December 17, 2011

Slip Away or Ship Aweigh

Shall I slip away, slip away
The phrase in memory played
Perhaps ship aweigh, ship aweigh
Was what I meant; over sighted

Slip away is idyllically
Meaning the lovers escapade
Done silent, surreptitiously
In poetry, abscondence made

While ship aweigh means boat movement
Not romantic for a sailor
Unless to ports known involvement
With local girls, asks a favor

So my phrase could mean both to me
I being a sailor of sorts
And at the same time, I could be
The man eluding marriage torts

December 17, 2011

Reflection Time

There are times like this when Twinkie and I
Want to sit in bed and hear our music
Its reflection time, the songs turned down low, aye
Perhaps a last poem or a song lyric

Sometimes I sit with eyes closed, just thinking
Twinkie asleep, she does no nighttime jobs
If a thought enters I may start inking
My note pad ready for love story sobs

But maybe it's not romantic pen time
A reverie of something lost or found
Something of importance, simply sublime
That I could fashion in poetic sound

And when finally I lay my head down
A smile of satisfaction on my face
I've got another poem worthy to own
A wonderful end of rapturous grace

December 19, 2011

Ever More

I'm a blue eyed poet
Born of the Norse god Thor
Christened using Moet
Heralded by a pagan whore
My name, ever lore

I shall write making sparks
My poems a fire will roar
With particles of quarks
Made only for making war
My creed, ever gore

In Sheol's chambers I dwell
Festering hate so sore
I ring the death note bell
From evil breasts hearts are tore
My goal, ever more

December 22, 2011

Forsaken

In Wrenwood City a ship did quay
Laden with cargo that none would say
Its presence unnoticed this fine day
Its portent of doom; as none would pray

Then in the quiet of evening rest
When families eaten of the best
There appeared, first seen towards harbors west
A glow, then sirens, it were no test

As firemen and rescue crews labored
The docks all dark in contrast quavered
Under passing of fire trucks neighbored
And in a spot distant, was savored

The people stunned asked why no warning
Was it caused by runaway barging
Then slowly at first, with barnstorming
A terrorist, much more alarming

First denied, then credit taken
The nation's people still were shaken
An obscure sect somewhere forsaken
Demanding a voice heard, now waken

December 23, 2011

At Dante's Tower

The world turns on your time
A second yours, a second theirs
So don't harp you of mime
The clock winds, its turning bears
Little of cares

For you thought it sped fast
When lust was on your breath
Did you stop, cry a vast
No, and then with death, the wreath
You place beneath

And now ask forgiveness
As if in my power
Pray, then in mine's finesse
For those at time that cower
At Dante's Tower

December 23, 2011

My Last Rose of Summer

My last rose of summer is a play on words
For Irish poet Thomas Moore, authored "The"
Last Rose of Summer, eighteen aught five records
And there have been countless songs written; ta da

My rose, a climbing yellow variety
Stayed long after its siblings vitality
Glowing in gorgeous sun liken majesty
Almost like it wanted no finality

So too have I enjoyed living its fullest
Ever continuing to give friendship life
To be in blossom for eternity, lest
I die like the flower and siblings so rife

This then is my Christmas gift I honor with
A yellow rose to remain ever blooming
A symbol of love and happiness so troth
On Christmas Day and New Year ever proving

December 24, 2011

Those Subtle Changes

The loss of my wife was a serious blow
It has changed my life, some subtle, some profound
The profound ways are easily explained how
It's those subtle changes I wish to expound

I write poetry; not every now and then
But in prolific numbers; I count them all
Averaging three per day with no end
These poems are not simple, child like, not withal

Another subtle change is my listening
I hear ideas that were once only noise
I read poems that before were only bristling
My uses of words, phrases and rhymes more wise

I have a gift; a friend said its channeling
That I'm being guided I'll not dispute here
The source of spontaneity not being
God, my late wife, cat Twinkie, a foreigner

Rather I believe a chemical changing
Some neurons of the brain, a permutation
Maybe a key turned, lock undone, opening
Whatever, but something changed; inspiration

I shall continue writing my poems at home
For maybe sometime soon or later, it ends
And if that happens I shall be so blithesome
I'll gather poems, publish, and retire my pens

December 25, 2011

Ink, Pen, and Paper

How wonderful the invention, ink
It lets one put down the forgotten
Those thoughts you hold in innermost sync
That place deep down where dreams are gotten

Then there is that instrument called pen
The holder of fluid soon to harden
Quill of old to newest plastic then
It's the writer, the keeper; warden

What of me; to see you need paper
I'm the holder of deeds most profound
The wheels of commerce, soon to taper
And all then to memorize; confound

I, the holder of pen and ink write
On paper the visions of grandeur
The ideas of prophet insight
Yes, all this recorded to endure

December 25, 2011

Day Dreaming

I tire not of day dreaming about
Floating memories, rudderless love
Such pleasure; my feelings show, are out
Nothing, save death, can deny me of

To recall with clarity my youth
Of days I spent without a worry
Walking to school, for to tell the truth
Those moments last, even books carry

I can be on safari hunting
Or driving a race car at Le Mans
Giving acceptance speech with bunting
Celebrating engagement at banns

I take the wind, advantage at sea
The bow smartly cutting through the blue
Even when death comes knocking for me
I close my eyes, day dreaming of you

December 23, 2011

A Silly Rhyme

Addle baddle caddle daddle
A monkey in a well so deep
Effle feffle geffle heffle
I threw him a locket to keep

Ittle jittle kittle little
A Rooster in a green Pine tree
Moddle noddle oddle poddle
My love note dropped she doth see

Qaddle raddle saddle taddle
A snarly dog has bone to eat
Uaddle vaddle waddle yaddle
I gave him something for his feet

Yoddle zoddle bingo busto
My poem is ended with the Z

December 26, 2011

A Poet's Daydream

A poet's daydream for all to see
Is written with love most tenderly
Of postures that only lovers be
Twixt pathos and rapture endlessly

Of pathos his daydream doth assuage
With words offered in sincerity
That they converse with clement usage
Thus seeking their mutuality

And of rapture his daydreams enthrall
For no greater state can lovers give
Than when apart they fondly recall
Those amorous moments they did live

December 26, 2011

She Comes a Twittery Way

She comes a twittery way
Skipping along, care free now
Like young maidens at play
Her pony-tailed hair alive with blow
Asking me, show

My eyes with tears not showing
Admiration with holding
Sternly, she'd think then knowing
Grandpa's a fraidy cat and scolding
No, extolling

I'm such a fuddy-duddy
She sees right through me I sense
Wanting to be her buddy
Oh how I wish, I'd give my essence
Not to be tense

My grandchild distantly lives
With visits much less often
My heart so readily gives
All that I can, but never mention
Tears, forgotten

December 26, 2011

They Buried My Soul Yesterday

Listen, they buried my soul yesterday
Not even a large gathering of folk
Likely spill over from another fresh lay
Perhaps the flowers drew them; yellow yolk

And such an interesting group there was
A few fresh minds, not tampered with at all
Some older of course, the forgotten cause
I even spied a devil too, such gall

There wasn't even a litany said
Some were wearing the absence of color
A fitting tribute, I thought, to the dead
For I'd laid myself out; cost a dollar

Afterwards, mourners left in twos and threes
Solemn, I'd provided no lunch for them
And in weeks, the leaves will fall from the trees
Covering what's left of my soul; amen

December 27, 2011

In God's Eye Equal

Sparrow lay dead upon the snow
I saw it stark as black on white
A cold reminder of winters blow
Producing that little birds plight

I wondered, did its consort know
Was it mourning or unaware
Perhaps it lay dead, covered now
Sparrows caught in Boreas' lair

Does God in infinite wisdom
Know of all creatures not human
Every Queen Cat and feral Tom
Every Hummingbird and Toucan

Then surely a Sparrows dead rest
Is noted; doth it please Him all
As spring thaws decay provides grist
For maggots, in God's eye equal

December 27, 2011

Lover's Kisses

It's not fair, you leaving me
Can't you see the spot I'm in
Who's going to make them tea
And cookies to bake, making them thin
With rolling pin

I'm not the cook like you were
Everything perfectly set
What tea cups and dinnerware
Are the cookies passed or do I let
Them ask first yet

Oh, I'll get everything done
It won't be easy either
Seeing that you were the one
Who orchestrated this party here
Your theater

Well, the guests have all gone home
Left me with dirty dishes
A poet might write a poem
In it he'd say; give me true wishes
Lover's kisses

December 27, 2011

Believe Thou Me, the Trinity

I've spoken with God in hushed words
Accept me now for what I am
A crooner with tired vocal cords
A poet who's not worth a damn

Before I could add anymore
He stopped me right there in my tracks
I was told, there's no need to score
As you are not judged by point racks

Your singing pleases many here
It's the timbre of your voice heard
That resonates with inner ear
But don't grow that goatee like beard

As for your poems, He said; write on
You enjoy a special gift there
And poems you rhapsodize will spawn
Many a lovers tryst so fair

And let me continue our talk
I judge a person's intention
Is it made to help others walk
Their own pathway to salvation

For even the poor and infirmed
Can ensure their way home to me
My place there is always confirmed
Believe thou Me, the Trinity

December 27, 2011

As if She'd Been Liable

A tear slowly made its way down her face
A perfect pose trying to smile her best
No one would even notice that her case
Had been heard, argued and judged on her tryst

The audacity to call it major
What he had done was much more terrible
Taking their home, his love and his honor
To spite her as if she'd been liable

Maybe someday a woman's voice could be heard
To be an equal with them, to have rights
There had been talk, whispers; only rumored
In America they heard women's plights

I wonder where they will take me now; bound
Prison life here can be very onerous
No matter, for in a week I'll be stoned
I will pray to God; they say He's gracious

December 28, 2011

You're a Crooner Mister T

You're a crooner Mister T
A latter day Bing Crosby
Well, not exactly, but gee
You make those older remember, sigh
Better times fly

And it's not your voice per se
That's a little weak on highs
A gentle tremolo, hey
That rattles their rafters, makes those cries
Swallowed, but ayes

And something else is present
You feel the mood of the song
And that is projected; sent
Feeling your memories, stored so long
That can't be wrong

December 28, 2011

I've Wrote in Poems

I've wrote in poems of love, of death, of hope
Of some dolor so great I cried and cried
Others they spoke rapture so great I swooned
But hope became nexus of life complete

I've wrote too of singing, laughing, praying
Of sounds, lyrics that make my heart quiver
Then too laughter of things silly season
And last of prayer to God humble remorse

I've wrote little of war, of peace, questions
As bombs dropped down, Vietnam, the scars remain
Wishing anger would end so frail accords
Seeking the truth, asking myself, answers

I've wrote at last Christmas, weather, my cat
Hung up holly, angels, colored tree lights
Seasons of rain, of drought, snow fall and heat
With her, Twinkie, bed mate, my pal, for life

December 29, 2011

Five Senses

I have seen the beauty of the Veldt
Where green and brown decide who is right
And if by casual observance felt
Evenings chill, then brown it is by night

I have taste the breeze from far off seas
Each tang of brine tells of origin
Salinity, the measure of these
Is different each ocean region

I have touched the ground upon I stand
Coarseness I feel tells of where it came
And moist or dry, I know of which land
And if pressed I will tell you its name

I have smelled the fragrance of flowers
Each species unique with its own smell
Place where you wish in garden bowers
I'll tell of Daisy, Sage and Bluebell

I have heard the trill of unseen bird
And from that very distinct sound, the name
Of its Genus and species inferred
When told the area which it came

December 30, 2011

The Irish

What is it about the Irish
That makes me want to be one
I like red hair; she's a dish
But then too is brown or black or blond
Pick one, I'm done

I suppose it's the music
Whether song or dance or jig
That gets my heart to beat quick
The lilt of Irish women, I dig
So shake a leg

A sentimentalist I
To trivialize, no sir
Within my soul there's a cry
Of freedom to live and not incur
Any rancor

December 31, 2011

About the Author

Stanley Paul Thompson has continued writing poetry since the publications of his first two books; *Sonnets of Life Well Spent* and *Troth & Rapture- 400 Sonnets*. Of the nearly 5,200 poems that he has written he has selected 124 of his earliest poems for this book.

A retired Naval Officer and pilot of carrier jet aircraft, he flew 114 combat missions in Vietnam. He received his Master's degree in Meteorology at the United States Naval Postgraduate School in Monterey, California. He has taught college mathematics, statistics, oceanography and naval history at four separate universities

He continues his life writing poems about everyday events; traveling the country in a new Lance trailer, visiting coffee cafés and bookstores, watching trains (an activity that his wife has encouraged), gardening, observing birds and animals and his many volunteer activities.

Mr. Thompson resides in Southern New Mexico with his wife, Karen, her dog Snickers and his cat Seylah Jane.

www.ingramcontent.com/pod-product-compliance
Lightning Source LLC
LaVergne TN
LVHW041251080426
835510LV00009B/696